EXTENDED WORSHIP

From The Heart Of A Worshiper

ETHEL L. COMER

Extended Worship; From the Heart of a Worshiper
Ethel L. Comer
Copyright © 2017. All Rights Reserved.
Author contact info: 6621 Winchester Rd., Ft. Wayne, IN
46819-1524. wmterryterrry@aol.com, (260) 403-0536.

Published by:
Anointed Words Publishing

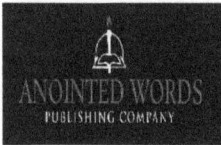

All Rights Reserved. No part of this book may be used or
reproduced in any manner whatsoever without the expressed
written permission of the author. Address all publishing inquiries
to:
2344 Shawnee Rd., #109
Lima, OH 45805
Email: awpubco@gmail.com
www.awpubco.com

ISBN: 978-1-947558-00-7
Printed in the United States of America
Scriptures marked KJV are taken from the KING JAMES
VERSION (KJV): KING JAMES VERSION, public domain.

DEDICATION

To Wings of Deliverance Tabernacle Holiness Church Praise and Worship team members: Eddie and Shelia Anderson, Linda Jones Brenda Boerger, Angelic Thomas, Robert Austin, Gerris Kelsaw, Eloise Scales, Chequitta Cowherd and Alexis Thomas and future worshipers.

To the Holy Spirit (without whom none of this would be possible); two wonderful parents, the late Samuel and Elizabeth Willis who, with the help of God, reared me to be a woman who loves God and family; for this, I am blessed beyond measure and eternally grateful.

To my dearest friend and sister, the late Fannie Beasley, my twin, Hester Brown, other siblings, living and those deceased. To Mother McDaniel, my Mentor, and my very supportive husband, Terry, I thank God for you and want you to know that my love for you is forever; I love you all.

To my daughters; Kimberly, and Natasha, my granddaughter, Tia; my son, Ron, who kept telling me, "Mom" you can do it; to my other children and ALL my "Spiritual" children (too many to list all by name), you all have made me feel as if I should have won the "Best Mom" Award. I have loved being a part of your maturation and overall productive lives watching how God is using so many of you in HIS service. Of course, I could not forget my other grands and great grands. I am praying that the legacy of loving God first and foremost will become and remain strong in each of you. I am so excited about what each of you will ultimately become!

To special friends; Bernice Bacon, Charlene Carr, Eloise Scales, Sam O'Neal; to Yvette Graham, Pastor Diane Allen-Bennett, Lady Lahoma (all Spiritual daughters); to Pastor Rhonda Bolden, who kept telling me years ago to "write the book; do not die with it inside of you," I thank you!

Lastly, but certainly not any less important, my church family, Wings of Deliverance Tabernacle Holiness Church. I thank God for my late Pastor, Bishop Jimmie C. Clark, Sr., Mother Marilyn Clark, and all other officers and prayerful congregation.

To my present Pastor, Robert and Lady Alesha Clark; thank you both for pushing me to the limits of my Worship, and for reminding me that whatever the assignment given, when God ordains it, remember your response must be: "I can do all things through Christ which strengtheneth me." Philippians 4:13 (KJV)

To Rita Fagin, professionally known as, "simply rita," (and another Spiritual daughter), thank you for your expertise and countless hours that you so willingly gave as you worked tirelessly to get the book ready for publication. I thank you for your professionalism, meticulous nature, and love.

Pastor Sherrick Anderson, thank you for agreeing to be part of this endeavor without a second's hesitation in writing the "Foreword."

CONTENTS

FOREWORD

The ultimate goal of this book is to give insightful revelation about Praise with a priority on taking Worship to a deeper degree. The writer, my "Spiritual Mom," Ethel L. Comer, has written what the Spirit revealed to her what Extended Worship (From the Heart of a Worshiper) is from her heart, which is that of a Worshiper. As I read its contents, I am happy to say that even though I am not a "well-known" author, television personality, and all the usual titles from whence a "Foreword" comes, I am a born-again believer, Pastor, and Worshiper and am grateful for the privilege of being able to know her and call her my "Mom" all these years. I am thankful for her ministry and most appreciative of the Lord for giving her the boldness to write the book.

This book is one that tells what some don't know, while others might, but just don't apply. The contents will bring to light in some instances, stir up the desire to go beyond in other instances, and also will cause you to know that at no time is your Worship about you.

She begins with a little background as to her rearing and how hesitant she was about placing on paper what the Spirit revealed to her. She is literally pleading this as the book is read. It is done without judgment, but with openness of heart to be able to receive what she received through revelation.

I felt the inner struggle she encountered in putting on paper what she felt in her spirit person. Extended Worship (From the Heart of a Worshipper) is a must-read; you will discover the depth of Worship in a way not perceived possible; this is what happened to me, yes, a Pastor. I really liked the way "Mom" broke down the difference between Praise and Worship, and how they are to be used in service, and the true significance of both.

My heart was touched from the section on men, and how God is looking for those who are not afraid to Worship. I enjoyed the personal touch shared where she was pushed into a place where Worship became her sustainer when attacked with a Cecal Mass (cancer) in her colon. The heartbeat of the writer, Ethel L. Comer, is Extended Worship. She has shared this with you in order to ignite a greater desire in each of you to WORSHIP.

Pastor Sherrick Anderson,
Higher Ground Church-Beloit, WI.

ACKNOWLEDGEMENTS

When the Holy Spirit impressed upon me to write this book, I admit it was a project that I felt was unattainable since I was a novice when it came to writing material for publication. I went into agonizing mode as I began to realize how much research, communication with others, and sheer dedication it would take to see this come to fruition. It took years to complete, but thanks be to God all the components came together for the completion of the book.

I was not privy to have people contribute their time to assist in the assembling and editing of this work in great detail (other than Rita Fagin), but I acknowledge heartfelt thanks to those individuals who stood in the gap for me in prayer to make this amazing, thought-provoking, and Holy-Spirit inspired piece a reality. If anyone would like to correspond with me, you may contact me at:

Heart of a Worshipper Evangelist Ethel L. Comer, 6621 Winchester Rd., Ft. Wayne, IN 46819-1524. wmterryterrry@aol.com (260) 403-0536.

My words to each person is to keep pursuing, keep pressing, keep persevering, keep lifting HIM up, then allow HIM to raise you up to where HE is and refuse to be ordinary in WORSHIP; instead, become extraordinary as you are transported into the very presence of an Omnipotent, Omnipresent, Omniscient, and Transcendent God!

I thank each of you beforehand for allowing me to enter into your lives through the reading of this book.

INTRODUCTION

Growing up in the South in a large family it was just commonplace to hear prayer, singing going forth, and just trusting God was a way of life; being a part of such a family, we amused ourselves by "playing" church. One sibling would preach, some would sing, and I was always the one who sang and danced in what I called "the Spirit" even though at the time, I had no idea what it actually meant.

While other kids were playing, we were memorizing the 23rd Psalms, John 3:16, Matthew 6:9-13 (called "The Lord's Prayer,") and Psalm 34:1. Even though we knew these and was able to recite them, what really stayed foremost in my mind, even at an early age, was "how do I really WORSHIP God?" I traveled to many cities and states with one of my aunts to "conventions" and listened intently to the term, "devotion."

As churches grew in many ways, the term changed to "Praise and Worship." I was mesmerized by the Worship and began to read everything I could get my hands on relating to "TRUE WORSHIP." I was reluctant to speak about the many, many thoughts on the subject to others, but as time passed, and as I grew into womanhood, the tug was on me to write a book about it, (especially during the time of the attack on my body, which will be discussed later). However, all I kept saying was, "No one wants to read another book on Worship." I mentioned it to Sam (my brother-in-love), along with my deceased sister and "bestest" friend, Fannie.

During the time I was talking to them, God kept speaking in my inner spirit to tell others what the Spirit had shown me about WORSHIP. Finally, I became obedient and began writing.

Psalms 96:9 (KJV) states: "O worship the Lord in the beauty of holiness: fear before him, all the earth." Just seeing the word WORSHIP intrigued me then as now. I literally became engrossed in finding out what the Word of God had to say about it for myself. I found that the importance of regular WORSHIP is expressed in scripture some 8,629 times.

As you read the book, ask the Spirit in every part, to open the eyes of your understanding to grasp what has been given to me through revelation and actually visiting the Throne Room in a visitation in 2013. I cannot say for certain if it was a vision or a dream, but this is what I was shown:

"I saw Him, God, sitting on the seat in Heaven with Jesus on his right side and angels repeatedly bowing before them crying, "Holy, Holy, Holy." No, I did not see either of their actual faces, but I knew that I was in the presence of such stupendous greatness and power that I, too, had to bow and lay prostrate before the throne. What was so strange was that I could look back to earth and see my body lying next to my husband who was still asleep in our bed.

As I kept lying there, I dared to raise my eyes a little and was almost blinded by the brilliance of such majesty and splendor right before me! I glanced down at his feet; the feet that had been nailed to the cross and still showed the imprint of where the nails had been driven. As my eyes traveled upward, I glanced at open hands with nail prints which also were still vividly apparent.

Being in total awe and reverence of where I was, I felt an inhibition to keep glancing upward. I crawled up from the prostrate position to one of kneeling and, with tears flowing down my cheeks, I heard a melodious, yet powerful voice sounding as if crossing many, many waters as he firmly, yet lovingly said:

"Daughter, I have allowed you to see this not to elevate YOU in and of yourself, but for you to go back carrying with you a greater revelation of what AUTHENTIC WORSHIP is. Tell all who will listen and those who even refuse to, that there IS a difference between Praise and Worship. Tell them I seek to find the heart of the True Worshipers. The voice kept talking and said, I am entrusting you to lead, by example, what AUTHENTIC WORSHIP is; I have both called and chosen you to be a Living Worshiper."

I came out of the state I was in with a "Yes, Lord, I will do it," and re-entered my still asleep body next to my husband.

CHAPTER 1 - PRAISE

Throughout scripture, you will find an impelling cry for people to PRAISE the Lord. If you pay close attention, nothing is mentioned telling anyone that he or she has to have a relationship with the Lord to do this. On the contrary, you will find it simply states in Psalms 150:1-6 (KJV): "PRAISE ye the Lord." Praise God in his sanctuary; praise him in the firmament of his power; praise him; praise him for his mighty acts; praise him according to his excellent greatness, praise him with the sound of the trumpet; praise him with the psaltery and harp, praise him with the timbrel and dance; praise him with stringed instruments and organs; praise him upon the loud cymbals; praise him upon the high sounding cymbals; let everything that hath breath praise the Lord. Praise ye the Lord."

We find that to Praise simply means to "Yadah" or plainly stated, "To give thanks." It is safe to say then that when scripture said, "Let everything that has breathe praise," this took into account all breathing creatures, correct? Praise is available to the angels (Psalms 148:2); it is available "TO" God's people (Psalms 8:2), but

NOT limited to them. It is available to children, adults, (Psalms 30:4); in short, all are summoned to praise God, (Psalms 67:3).

Going further than on the human side of Praise, God gives a directive for even inanimate nature to PRAISE him. This is referring to things such as the sun, moon, stars, (Psalms 148:3-4); fire, hail, snow, and even the wind, (Psalms 148:8); the mountains, hills, rivers, and yes, the mighty seas (Psalms 98:7-8). He even included the trees in his quest for praise unto him as found in (Psalms 148:9; Isaiah 55:12); ALL living creatures are to praise him (Psalms 69:34, and 148:100); all from the (KJV).

I repeat, nowhere in scripture text does it require a person to be saved to Praise. St. John 4:24, however, lets us know: "God is a spirit, and they that WORSHIP him must WORSHIP him in spirit and in truth."(KJV). There IS a difference!

It is crucial not to ignore Praise because it is a prelude to the HIGHER form of Praise which I call, WORSHIP. Therefore, you should commend, applaud, and magnify God as you give him thanks for the things he has done. You accomplish this by doing what David wrote in

Psalms 100:4, (KJV): "Enter into His gates with thanksgiving, and into his courts with praise: be thankful unto him, and bless his name." What David is asking here is for you to have a "Thank you, Lord" on your lips and gratefulness in your heart; for even the sinner can be thankful for what is given to him or her.

As Praise relates to songs that are sung by a Praise Team (in line with Psalms 100:4), the first song should be one which expresses one's thankfulness toward God. When you come through the gates (which I see as the initial entrance into the grounds before entering the sanctuary), you should take your time as you enter, focusing totally on letting God know how thankful you are for all that he has done, and even for what you expect him to do.

Once you are in the sanctuary and the Praise has begun, the Praise and Worship Team should never attempt to enter into WORSHIP until enough time has been given to thank God by joyful singing, proper music, clapping of the hands, and dancing in jubilation as you express how overwhelmed you are by God's goodness and kindness toward you. In Praise, there is a development or process that should be adhered to before attempting to go directly into the presence of the Father, God, by way of WORSHIP.

The same way, as in the natural, that you would not just barge into another person's home; you should use this same concept and not attempt to enter into the Holy of Holies prior to completing, then going to that phase of PURE WORSHIP. This comes after you have participated in Praise and are moved, by the Spirit, to go higher. God should not be short-changed because of other pending programs, offering, announcements, or just lack of sincere understanding in this area; God wants us to exhaust the Praise before moving on.

Praise-Team Leaders, this is key; do NOT become impatient, or in a hurry to the point whereby the people are not allowed to enter into HIS gates with thanksgiving; they should be allowed to get their thanks out before they are shut down. If the Praise is incomplete, many times what should be WORSHIP (to be discussed later), will turn into nothing more than a "what God has done for you dissertation" when the focus should only be on GOD.

When we are premature in our expression of Praise (which is just saying thanks), the manner of participation, as to what to do, when, and how to do it in the sanctuary seems to get confusing as directives are given. There HAS to be both clarity and ample time for progression; a forward movement before attempting to enter into God's presence for the "ACT" of WORSHIP. I stated this before, but it bears repeating, you CANNOT just charge in like a "bull in a china shop." Too often the entire move of the service is thrown off because a proper foundation of PRAISE (thankfulness, gratefulness) was NOT laid, nor was enough time spent in the courtyard just Praising him before moving forward.

I realize that some of this will be a learned experience because Praise and Worship has been breathed in the same breath, if you will, and linked together for so long that it is hard to differentiate. Also, this may be a learned experience because there are varied backgrounds in ethnicity, race, color, creed, demographics and, more importantly, church-background experiences.

You bring over how it was done wherever your prior attendance was and, while all of these are factors, the predominant factor MUST be for you to be willing to "wait" before moving on, and then be prepared to adjust to how the Praises should flow before going into WORSHIP.

CHAPTER 2 - MUSICIANS

Harmony should exist between the Praise and Worship Team Leader, its members, and people on the instruments so cohesively that it comes across as a fine-tuned instrument making beautiful music together. Also, when possible, the Praise and Worship should especially coincide with the message of the Pastor, or other speakers to determine, after praying about it, what songs will be relevant to what is to be ministered. This is not always possible, but being in constant concentration and prayer will always keep the leaders on point in this area.

I stress this, not as a criticism, but of importance, because when it isn't, one can unconsciously sing or play a song that will throw the entire atmosphere of the service off for those in charge. One wrong directive to the members can, and many times have thrown off the service.

It is important to be sensitive to the timing of your actions. What do I mean? Don't just "say" something to move the service along because you feel you have to, or this is what always has been done; be sure it is in line with what the Spirit is doing. Praise time is truly the time for the demonstrative acts of dancing, yelling, clapping, running, and screaming, but it is NOT the intent to remain indefinitely in the "outer court." A service is NOT a service if you have not touched God with your WORSHIP (to be discussed in further detail later).

The main focus of this book is NOT so much on PRAISE, but WORSHIP; however, in order to bring out what was opened up to me about Worship, it was necessary to discuss, in part, Praise because the two play an integral part in any service, but should NOT be used interchangeably, flipping back and forth, here one minute on Praise, then back to Worship. Praise is a key component in transitioning to what I call the HIGHER form of expressing your love and devotion to God, which is what I see as WORSHIP. This is the goal. This is your final destination

As you continue giving God a "never-the-less" praise with adulations of thank you; you are automatically led to a greater depth of how to honor the Lord. The more the Spirit reveals AUTHENTIC WORSHIP to me, I literally feel like crying (and sometimes do) when I observe honest, sincere, and meaningful hearts Praising, but, then when told to WORSHIP could not, would not, or just did not know how to transition because he, or she, felt there was no difference so why stop what was being done?

I weep when I see the disparity in understanding the role and order of each; not as a put-down, but a feeling of lack of teaching, and many times correct example in this area.

Hopefully, the revelation the Spirit has given me will help us all arrive at a place of being able to differentiate, with the aid and inspiration of the Holy Spirit, what, and how both should be done. By no stretch of the imagination is it a sin to intermix the two, but when it occurs, it does cause the service to be topsy-turvy.

Some statements of nothing but Praise are listed below. These sound good, and are true, but should NOT be used once the movement of the service has shifted from Praise to Worship. Why? These statements turn it all back on YOU; what YOU have received, and is not about HIM, or his sovereignty!

"Lord, I thank you for waking me;" "I thank you for

health and strength;" "I thank you for shelter and food;"

"I thank you for family and friends;"

I thank you for giving me a sound mind and body;" "I thank you for peace;"

"I thank you for the job that I have;"

"I thank you for the job you will give me;"

"I thank you that I live in a land where I am free to praise;" "I thank you for those who have rule and authority over me so that I might lead a quiet and peaceful life."

"I thank you for healing and saving me."

The list could go on and on, but while we should articulate these, they should be used when Praising. When we Praise, the focus really is on "SELF." It is, or SHOULD be all about what God has done "FOR" you. It is both thankfulness and appreciation for the "works" God has performed that benefited YOU in one way or another. It is about what was done on YOUR behalf. PRAISE is broad, but yet basic. It causes you to be filled with a particular mood or tone. It is all-inclusive to the entire world; not limited to anything, nor anyone. Praise is very much needed.

One might ask, "What exactly is the position, or attitude of Praise? Its position is one of constant activity. It is perpetual motion as participators run, clap, and yell. It tends to be loud, but not all the time, and certainly not with music that is always fast (as believed by many when relating to Praise). This concept of Praise is an erroneous thought and is definitely misleading to those often in charge of Praise and Worship, as well as onlookers.

Many people have the perception that Praise is indicative of a "fast" song, and if it isn't fast, they believe there was NO Praise. No! This thought is a fallacy! To know if the song is a "Praise" song, listen to the song's lyrics; are the words citing thanks and gratefulness to God? If the answer is, "yes," then that is a "Praise" song. It is the words of the songs that perpetuate Praise regardless of the tempo of the music.

While Praise does allow you to vent your emotions, you need to press to a HIGHER place, and that is WORSHIP. The activity of Praise makes you "feel" good emotionally, but you must pursue more. It is true that God wants everything that has breath to praise, but you have to go farther and enter into WORSHIP. If you miss the shift and move outside of HIS timing, you throw the entire service out of alignment. I cannot stress enough how important this is.

If in your Praising you could just remember that it is NOT your final destination, but that the primary goal is to end up in the Throne Room (through your Worship), then you might be more prone to "press" in harder to get there. It is only mature people and those who understand the power of WORSHIP who will comprehend this. It is only those who understand that there IS a significant difference between the two who keep praising, persevering, and are ready to move into WORSHIP. However, if this is not fully understood right now, do NOT become disheartened nor despondent, you will gain this understanding as you continue to read this book.

Before I end the section on Praise, I want to include some Biblical words and brief definitions of Praise:

Halal- *to talk about with pride; to be merry; to celebrate God.*

Tehillah- *to express esteem or admiration for; to brag on Him.*

Shabach- *to say with a loud voice; to shout victory praises to God.*

Zamar- *to sing and praise using various types of instruments.*

Yadah- *to raise the hands upward to God as one speaks verbal thanks to Him.*

Towdah- *to raise the hands in thanksgiving with deep, passionate, intense, and enthusiastic thanks to God.*

Barak- *to bend low as you accept the fact that God is superior to you.*

Shachah- *to bring low; debase your attitude of "self" and turn your focus toward God; to celebrate with an expressed attitude of the heart.*

These forms of PRAISE show up in the service before entering into WORSHIP. The Praise should continue until a "spirit" of WORSHIP sits in the room; it should never stop just to "get on with the service." This statement is important because those persons who have that personal relationship with God, and who are blood washed and regenerated will begin to experience a "shift" in their inner person and will notice a "pulling" in the spirit that it is time to go deeper, higher, and closer to HIM. Only those people will be able to do this genuinely.

When this happens, this is the indication that something else is about to happen; everyone needs to be willing to abandon whatever has been taking place to get in the position to give way to the anticipated presence of someone more phenomenal. At this juncture, all should be getting ready to go to the HIGHER level of Praise as the Spirit groans AND yearns for that elevated form known as WORSHIP.

CHAPTER 3 – WORSHIP EXTENDED

When you hear the word, WORSHIP, just what do YOU think about? Well, from experience and talking to many people, it is, as I stated earlier, regarded as a "slow" song. WORSHIP is so much, more than a slow song sung by a Praise team or choir; it is neither the largest giver, the one who is at every service, the one with the greatest talent, the best organizer, the one who volunteers to do whatever needs to be done at the church, the oldest, or most faithful member.

"To WORSHIP" is to make alive your awareness of the Holiness of God. It is to feed your mind with the truth of God; to cleanse the imagination by the awesomeness of God; to love God with a heart that is open; and to give up YOUR will totally to pursue the purpose of God."

In my research, I found quite a few definitions for the word, but the one which stood out foremost was found in Webster's Dictionary, 1828 which stated: "WORSHIP is to honor with extravagant love and extreme submission." In other words, as Worship relates to God, it is to esteem HIM higher than anyone or anything. He is loved beyond measure, and your lives are totally submitted to HIM above all else. Praise God!

EXTENDED WORSHIP is how we love, how we live, how we give, how we speak and treat others; these all depict TRUE WORSHIP. It transcends the mere act of "feeling" good when a slow song arouses emotions within but yet, you are walking outside of love. This type of mindset is not WORSHIP in spirit and in truth, and God is NOT accepting this "tainted" gift!

True, Authentic WORSHIP is "God, you are the audience of one;" it is not about impressing anyone; in fact, when you enter into HIS presence all you should have eyes for is HIM! He becomes your top priority; you place "who" he is above "what" he has done for you, is doing for you, will do for you, or can do for you.

True Worship causes you to reflect on exactly where you are and, if the Worship is in place, the statement will be, "God, YOU take preeminence in my life because you are my Alpha and Omega; you are my beginning and my end. I permit you to have free reign as I WORSHIP you."

This WORSHIP being talked about is to share a revealed fact that it must be True and Authentic; it must be a lifestyle of Holiness. The term, "Holiness" has nothing to do with a person's denomination, how one dresses, or who is their pastor. It is a lifestyle that exemplifies the beauty of Holiness through a daily and "on-purpose" walk with God so that others may see CHRIST in not so much as what is said, but by what is shown in every area of one's life.

A person who is a True, Authentic Worshiper has a hunger to Worship God. A hunger to love on him; to honor him as being the one true and Sovereign Lord; the ONLY Supreme being, the Author and Finisher of our Faith, and we acknowledge and accept this completely without coercion because he IS God and he deserves our WORSHIP!

Psalms 96:9 (KJV) states: "O worship the Lord in the beauty of holiness: fear before him, all the earth." The word WORSHIP is mentioned some 8,629 times in the Bible; surely something mentioned that many times must be important, agreed?

When we get to the place where we realize that "God, it is YOU whom I have come to give my gifts to" instead of always coming to see what can be gotten, then a powerful revelation on WORSHIP will have been received.

One thing is certain; you will never out give the Father. If you just forget about "what have you done for me lately," and change the tune to: "All to Jesus I surrender," you will be able to enter in and just enjoy the wonders of being in the awesome presence of God in sincerity (and not merely pretending), or because others are prompting or watching.

To enter in, you must become sensitive to what is taking place and become so aware of the presence of God and how HE wants to move and not allow your PERSONAL agendas to dictate how the service will take place. Order is always appropriate, but at ALL times the Spirit of God must mandate the activity of any service; not the person officiating. It is time to forget about you and just enjoy God's eminence and reverence the fact that HE loves you so much that he blesses you with his divine presence as HE shows up to receive your gifts of WORSHIP.

One of my "spiritual daughters," Rita Fagin, pen-named, "simply rita," has beautifully touched the true essence of "Extended Worship" in this poem written by her:

EXTENDED

Extended from this heart of mine
A Worship in my soul
Expressions coming out of me
In moments in control
Uplifted to the arms of God
For Him and only Him
He gave to me the brightest light
Before it was so dim
It's true I praise the Lord above
In song or with a dance
But Worship shows another love
My spirit so enhanced
I silence that which may distract
And focus on the King
I saturate my face with tears
Among so many things
I bow in honor of the gift
In me, He chose to dwell
To me, He gave the great of greats
His Son Emanuel
In Worship, God begins to speak
He tells of what He sees
Sometimes corrections, better yet
He says He's very pleased,

I will lift my voice and clap my hands
In truth that is my start
And then will come, Extended love
And Worship from my heart

simply rita
Copyright© 2-15-17

CHAPTER 4 – WORSHIP MUSIC

When the position, or activity, of <u>WORSHIP</u> is visible, this is when the music needs to be adjusted. If the music was loud before, it now needs to be soft, calm, and serene. <u>This</u> is paramount! <u>If you keep pushing, prodding, and playing loud, fast, hard music, it is going to cause the mood to excite and emotionally charge the flesh, and the congregation will digress to running, dancing, and screaming; this action will take you right back to the OUTER courts; back to the gates and in the courtyard.</u>

I stress this because it grieves others and for <u>certain</u>, the Holy Spirit when HE has shown up and is moving on the hearts of True Worshipers. The Worshippers are on one accord, all are hailing the King, and they, the Worshipers, are at the place now where NO ONE and NOTHING else matters, and then you hear someone yell, "PRAISE HIM!"

While the intent is a good one, the intended move of the Spirit toward WORSHIP has now <u>been broken</u>. It is so important to know that when the glory of God falls, the service is no longer about you. When this type of command <u>is</u> <u>given</u>, even if well meant, that command takes the people back to concentrating on themselves!

The action of "feeling good" needs to take a back seat because it is now no longer the order of the day, and those who are Worshippers need to begin to pray for the service to stay in tune with the move of the Spirit. When the service is at this juncture, there is LITTLE or NO need to talk in an attempt to coerce anyone into doing anything. The Spirit should have full control here. If in doubt as to whether to <u>talk</u> or not, TRUST the Spirit; HE is <u>a good</u> person to be in charge, and most definitely knows the order.

If you will stay in tune with the Holy Spirit and continue to press in, you will begin to experience a feeling of "weight." <u>This</u> is the GLORY of the Lord; this is his "weighted presence;" this is the Kavod. When one moves out of order, whether accidentally or on purpose, it brings an awkwardness to the service and then the people do not <u>really</u> know what to do or where to go from that point because they are <u>totally</u> unaware of what has transpired. When this occurs, it also interrupts the work that the Spirit longed to do, and WAS doing through

WORSHIP.

This information given to me is in no way intended to be condescending in any manner; it is expressly <u>intended</u> to pass on only what the Spirit placed in my spirit and instructed me to share. <u>The words tells us in Hosea 4:6 (KJV): "My people are destroyed by the lack of knowledge," so until we get the distinct difference, and know His timing and how to react to PRAISE, then to WORSHIP, we will continue to interact out of order and, thus, continue to throw the service out of "spiritual alignment."</u>

The aftermath of moving out of order finds those in charge trying to get the congregation back to the place of entering into HIS presence. To add clarity, let me ask you, how many believe that there are 'seasons' to what Worship can do in a service? If you believe this to be true, then you must also believe that the timing must be right, and if people are encouraged to move OUT of the season of the Spirit, then you miss the Spirit's plans to heal, deliver, save, and restore.

The emphasis here is to move with the HOLY SPIRIT; to follow HIM! Likewise, I believe when you have entered a place in WORSHIP and then move out of that place too quickly, or throw a curve in it; you lose what you were to receive. It's true, you might be going through the motions, but are you really touching the heart of God? Are you really back where the Spirit had you? I think not.

It is so vital that those in areas of leadership (as it relates to WORSHIP) know that it is NOT something that can be "worked up," or "coerced" into doing. WORSHIP must be "entered" into through the Spirit. "God is a Spirit and they that worship him must worship him in spirit and in truth. John 4:24 (KJV). WORSHIP is pouring out of your soul, revealing the never-ending love you have towards a deserving GOD!

To fully Worship God, it is necessary to have a strong, intimate, relationship with him; intimacy--in-to-me-see. You need always to ask God to reveal who he is to you as an individual. Proverbs 20:27 (KJV) states: "The spirit of a man is the lamp of the Lord, searching all the inner depths of his heart." It is the "light;" it illuminates and then exposes the TRUE intentions of the heart.

AUTHENTIC WORSHIP will search out anything that is NOT like God in truth. Because you are unable to genuinely Worship God in the flesh, it is paramount that you purify yourself of WORLDLY thoughts, actions, and evil-related things in order for your spirit to WORSHIP God by HIS spirit.

WORSHIP must come from the place of a PURE heart; good as he, or she might be in appearance, those engaging in fornication, uncleanness, passion, evil desire, covetousness, which is idolatry CANNOT give God PURE WORSHIP: Colossians 3:5 (KJV) paraphrased. It is time to STOP asking God to cleanse you; you must cleanse yourself then WORSHIP God from a PURIFIED heart where NO flesh (regardless of how good the intentions may be) can reside.

Once you are free from anything you know is NOT of God, the part of your spirit that remains will then allow you to WORSHIP the Mighty Spirit of God, but not until you first die to your flesh! Flesh is an enemy of WORSHIP because flesh wants to be seen and is always seeking ways to "upstage" itself. This is why, as mentioned in the Praise section of this book, as good as you "feel" when you Praise, give it all you have at that allotted time, however when it is time to enter into WORSHIP, ALL the activities of PRAISE must CEASE because PRAISE is self- serving (about you), while WORSHIP is "God-centered;" all about HIM! Selah.

CHAPTER 5 – WORSHIP ACTIONS

As WORSHIPERS move into the manifested presence of God, many times, tears will begin to fall down the faces of those in Majestic Worship; others will sit quietly and every so often, a hand will go up toward heaven; some may even be lying prostrate on the floor in sheer honor of WHO God is, and how deserving he is without one thought about how he or she is perceived by onlookers.

You might be thinking, "this is weird, and why would anyone submit themselves to forgetting totally about what he or she is wearing and doing anything like this?" The answer is simple; being obedient to the Spirit and what He dictates. It is because the Worshipers realize that this is NOT, nor has it EVER been, nor will it EVER be about them, they are in the presence of God, and all else is now null and void, including people and what they think. This is no longer an important issue; they are TOTALLY immersed in HIM and aware only of the move of God as they stand in his presence.

The Worshiper is now completely lost in the

confines of their love for God and NOTHING else matters! In case anyone is wondering what has happened, you have stepped within the veil; you are now standing in the Holy of Holies. There are no words at this point to fully describe God's anointing power as you stand in His presence being fully liberated and blessed in whatever area where there is a need. Because of his magnificence, the Spirit has the power to move on whomever, and however HE so chooses. Because of this, you stand in awe of not only his omnipotence, but the fact that each Worshippers' "ACT" of Worship might be different from each other in nature and quality. Worshipping differently is okay as long as God, and God alone, gets the glory and it is decent and in order.

As noted before, some will bow, some will fall on their faces, and some will even go out in the spirit from this weighted presence. What an honor and a privilege it is to WORSHIP the Lord! In the midst of WORSHIP, there might be a word given in tongues; be careful here; be sure it is from the Spirit and not someone just enjoying congregational Worshipping and speaking only to HIM in their heavenly language of "secret" communication. In this action, there should be keen and lucid discernment by the person or persons, in charge to know if the tongue is a word to be shared through interpretation. Leaders should horn in on this as the speaker gets louder and the tongues become more spiritually defined.

If the Spirit has a message to the body, the leaders (and others in sync with the Spirit) should pick it up, as a quiet, hush falls in the sanctuary and the message is given. Bear in mind, however, that even this should always be done decently and in order and NEVER given in a disruptive or attention-getting manner. The giver will speak; not preach a message, but speak what thus says the Lord, then if the giver does not interpret, another person who has the gift of interpretation should give a "condensed" interpretation and not a mini-sermon. Again, neither of these actions demand the givers to draw attention to their person by screaming or other disruptive actions.

If NO interpretation is given, "flesh" has once again raised its head and brought about confusion in the body. A general rule of thumb, (in order to be in line with the move of the Spirit) is, "when HE shows up and takes complete charge of the service, flow WITH him; there is no reason for talking from any other source at that time."

There is such a reward in Worship! I am talking here about the "ACT;" your participation. You enter into thanksgiving and Praise at the onset of the service, but your desire should always be to "visit" the Father; to spend quality time just loving on him as he imparts, (without actual words, but by the Holy Spirit), great and precious revelations.

The Father requires Holiness, so you who go to him in the Holy of Holies must also "be" Holy; not by dress, church affiliation, or by a set of established rules of do's and don'ts; but with a LIFESTYLE. When the lifestyle and relationship is in place, all else will follow.

When you enter into PURE WORSHIP, things will emerge that will not surface otherwise. As the Spirit begins to minister to your spirit, you become empowered to be all that he pre-ordained you to be. This does not take place because "you" are so anointed, but it happens because of the place where you have gone, and that is in the very presence of a rewarding and gracious God.

To sit in His presence brings Spiritual

direction, renewed strength, and healing, to name a few. Worship causes you to step outside of the thoughts and limitations of the mind and allows the Spirit to take over. He then performs whatever needs to be reconstructed while you are in His presence if you are willing, submissive, and patient long enough for Him to do His work.

Observation and experience have revealed the fact that without actually owning up to it, many go to the Father "whipped" and "beaten" down by life itself. While WORSHIP is primarily about WHO God is, and our part is to love on Him, no loving Father will ever allow his children to pour "into" Him without reciprocating "TO" them.

Even as you are loving on Him, God so masterfully receives your "Extended Worship" as it becomes a "give-and-take" act of love. Yes, it is ALL about Him, but because of his love, his compassion, his empathy, it is just His nature to pour back into his children. When this "ACT" of WORSHIP has subsided, you find that even though you went in to remind Him how dear he is to YOU, wanting nor asking for anything in return; you leave refreshed, restored, renewed, regenerated, and re-committed; all because you dared to "linger" in the presence of God! Oh, God, how awesome are your ways; NONE can compare to your immeasurable and everlasting love. Thank you, Lord!

CHAPTER 6 - WORSHIP HINDRANCES

In conversations with people from various walks of life, some expressed the fact that they cannot enter into WORSHIP the way he or she might desire. Some asked, "why was it so easy, it seemed, for me to Worship?" The only response I could give was, "God had given me a heart for WORSHIP after developing a deep relationship with him, and I don't allow anything, nor anyone to cause me not to do so; (includes being ridiculed for my lifestyle of Holiness)."

Often when people come to WORSHIP they cannot because they come with a lot of unresolved issues; they come with hidden SITUATIONS that are weighing them down. To be perfectly honest, they are saved, but it is still a real struggle for them to even get to the house of God and, after having made it, they feel empty because they came needing to let go and allow God to do what HE is so capable of doing (freeing them of the things which had them bogged down), but such was not the case because when the service was over, no yokes had been destroyed and they went out as despondent and lost as when they entered (this should never be the case).

I write from a place of experience because I, too, have come to the house needing only to touch God; no fanfare, no gimmicks, just to touch Him, and I found I had to actually "press" my way because I had distractions getting in the way of my WORSHIP, and weights that I had brought in with me, tugging, whispering in my ear.

The following are some hindrances and, this is by no stretch of the imagination, meant to serve as all-inclusive of what comes to hinder your WORSHIP. It will give, however, a "bird's-eye view" of some things to be aware of when you find yourselves struggling with entering into that sacred place of WORSHIP. Some hindrances are:

Known and practiced sin, or weights; Spiritually, mentally, physically, or emotionally tired or drained;

Critical of everything and everyone in ministry; (those on the Praise Team, or those ministering the word).

Sidebar Note: To present your best in WORSHIP, you must be tolerant. If there is an identified mistake made, the position must be one of prayer; not criticism; no one always sings in perfect pitch, but ask yourself, "Am I here to critique the service, or to add to it by moving forward in my expression of WORSHIP to God?"

Lack of patience;

(This is a "definite" hindrance and is key. We will stand for hours to see a movie, concert, check-out lane for that outfit we just have to have, the after-Thanksgiving, "Black Friday" sales, but become noticeably irritable and restless if the WORSHIP goes longer than we think it should. We then begin talking, passing notes, rambling in our purses, and running to and from the bathroom; not talking about persons with medical problems.)

You MUST mature beyond these hindrances. Your FULL attention needs to be on what you can GIVE to God in your WORSHIP and not how long you wait, annoyed because the service went longer than desired, or expected. How do you know what the Spirit desired to do when you were not willing to hear from HIM?

WORSHIP is not the time to discuss where you plan to eat, who is ministering at night service, if you plan to come back, and, being brutally honest, I have been guilty of not just one, but a few of these. These statements are experiential! Whether guilty or never having done any of the list of hindrances, the point here is to STAY focused at ALL cost and refuse to dwell on anything, or anyone, BUT GOD!

I know Praise and Worship team leaders will shutter at what I am about to say, but it works to help deter me from hindrances to my WORSHIP. I found that when I close my eyes, I am able to actually visualize presenting my BEST gift of WORSHIP to God, and I am not drawn into any outside disturbances. (I try NOT to keep them closed 100% of my Worship time.)

When I am in the "PRAISE mode," I am able to comply with keeping my eyes open; however, as I move deeper into WORSHIP, without even realizing it, my eyes automatically close as I escape into a place where God and I are immersed, it seems, into one. My actions are by no means intended to be disobedient to authority, but my WORSHIP is personal; therefore, I must, as the Spirit leads, involve my entire being into it;

and if the only way to accomplish this is to close my eyes to eradicate distractions, then that is the route I take.

The contents of this book are by no stretch of the imagination intended to imply that it is the first and final say, as it relates to WORSHIP, but it does convey the revelations made to ME regarding the subject. I know that if read prayerfully and then applied, it will emerge you into a TRUE, AUTHENTIC WORSHIPER in all Biblical aspects of this mighty and powerful tool.

I realize there are hundreds of books and tapes out there about Praise and Worship, and that there will be, for certain, many more in the future as each person conveys what was given to him, or her the way the Spirit gave it. My writing was a direct mandate from the Holy Spirit. Getting it done became my passion; all that is contained herein is intended to widen the thoughts on WORSHIP and point you, the reader, to the ONLY person deserving of your WORSHIP and that is GOD ALMIGHTY!

CHAPTER 7 - A TRUE WORSHIPER

To be a "TRUE" Worshiper, there has to be a never-ending ache from within to experience, over and over, the deep love between you, the Worshiper, and God. The FIRST love must be with Jesus, and then with others, because if there is no love, your Worship is in vain.

True Worship restores the glory of God within you. What is a TRUE WORSHIPER?

A True Worshiper is one whose only goal is to please God;

A True Worshiper is NOT a "glory" seeker; does not need, nor solicit accolades from man;

A True Worshiper will ALWAYS go that extra distance to enter into the Throne Room;

A True Worshiper guards, at all times, the heart and makes sure the heart remains one of love.

A True Worshiper meets with God, face-to-face (in the spirit) daily; not just when it is time to enter the sanctuary.

A True Worshiper's life revolves around maintaining joy in spirit no matter the circumstances, issues, or problems. Why? Because nothing negates the fact that God is yet deserving of Worship.

A True Worshipers' DAILY lifestyle exemplifies stability in CHRIST and a LIFE of consecration!

Author's Disclaimer:

I have not arrived simply because you read the contents of this book, by no stretch of the imagination, is such the case; however, I KNOW what God expects from Christians, Believers, or Saints. (Whichever name you are called in the body.) I know further, that "when," not "if " you miss it, (and we ALL do), a True Worshiper does NOT gloss over the infraction to the Word of God, but immediately repents in order to rebuild and restore his, or her position for WORSHIP.

As I was writing, the Spirit sat heavily upon me to take the time to do a self-analysis to evaluate if I was clothed in the proper garments to be called, "A True Worshiper" over and above those listed. I am proposing that you do the same. The bar used for the self-evaluation is found in

Galatians 5:23-24 (KJV): "But the fruit of the Spirit is love, joy, peace, longsuffering, gentleness, goodness, faith, meekness, temperance: against such, there is no law."

When you are a True Worshiper, these nine (9) slices of "one" fruit should be active in your life as you give way to the Spirit to orchestrate and influence.

When the Holy Spirit inspired Paul to write Galatians, he also gave him the order that the fruit should be; he began with love, the foundation to everything. Let's look at each fruit and the characteristic of each that needs to be developed in each person if he or she, is to be a "True Worshiper:"

LOVE (Gr - agape) - When real love is in operation, you are not looking to reciprocate any type personal benefit; all you really want is what is best for others (whether they behave the way you think they should or not); real love loves the sinner, but not the sin unconditionally.

JOY (Gr - chara) - You maintain your joy regardless because it is based on what you possess inwardly (and not on circumstances, or feelings); so you keep Worshipping!

PEACE (Gr - eirene) - You are able to hold onto your peace because your heart and mind is constantly on God; this comes when you know him intimately and have a "real" relationship with him.

LONGSUFFERING (Gr - makrothumia) - You are consumed with a deeper level of patience with people; the shortcomings of others don't cause you to become angry easily; you show empathy and keep Worshipping despite, and against all odds.

GENTLENESS (Gr- chrestotis)-There is a genuine concern in how you treat others; you are consciously aware of how you speak, and are consciously attempting to not inflict pain.

GOODNESS (Gr- agathosune)-The question to "self" is, "Am I showing kindness to those who might be performing sinful, evil acts even though I am in no way placing a stamp of approval on his, or her actions? Am I continuing to care (with Godly compassion) as I continue my quest for righteousness and truth?"

FAITH (Gr - pistis) - You are committed, and standing firm, as you remain faithful to the promises of a reliable and dependable God.

MEEKNESS (Gr- prautes)- You have the power, through Christ, to keep anger under control even when situations warrant other action; you possess the ability to experience anger, but yet not sin; you do this (not in boasting or your strength), but in "humble obedience" to the word, and the strength of God.

TEMPERANCE (Gr - egkrateia) - You have control over yourself in areas of ambition, appetite; aspirations, and passions; ALL things are kept in "Biblical balance."

It is 100% true that NONE of "us" will hit the mark in ANY areas 24/7, but it should be the goal of every Worshiper; to go through the process to attain these attributes, and then maintain them (which is the mark for which all should be striving to reach).

Extended Worship (From the Heart of a Worshiper) was birthed in my spirit to let all know that it HAS to surround you; it has to be "more than just a slow song." It HAS to be portrayed in ALL of the above-listed areas if the Worship is going to be True and Authentic. The key word here is, EXTENDED. You must allow WORSHIP to get out of that finely-wrapped package that it has been kept in far too long.

When the Spirit first impressed upon me to add this section to the book, my first thought was, "God, how in the world can I do this when we ALL miss it?" The question is no longer a big factor in my life because even when we miss the mark, we have a means of getting back on track and that is by SINCERE repentance; this gets us ALL back on course and allows us all to be TRUE WORSHIPERS!

CHAPTER 8 – HOW IMPORTANT IS WORSHIP TO YOU?

Co-authors of a book entitled, "Praise and Worship- Becoming Worshippers of God" (A. & Joyce Gill) stated, "There is a principle of Biblical interpretation called, "Law of Much Mention." This principle implies that the amount or quantity of space or time given a particular topic depicts the importance of that particular thing. I included this because of how many times the word, WORSHIP is mentioned directly, or indirectly in both the Old and New Testament; because of the repetitiveness of the word, this brought about this section, "How important is your Worship since it is apparently important to God?"

Is it important enough for you to forget about the time when in service and concentrate on the actual aspect of Worship? Is it important enough for you to ignore all distractions in order to enter into the presence of God? Is it important enough for you to become disciplined enough to cause your mind to be completely centered ONLY on the things of God? Is it important enough for it to be a LIFESTYLE to you? If you answered, "Yes," you are at the place where you need to be as it relates to how important it is to you; however, if you said, "No," then your mindset must change concerning Worship and needs to be broadened beyond the mere "ACT." Worship has to be entered into with total and complete abandonment in every sense of the word; Worship is getting rid of "self;" Worship requires sacrifice! Extended Worship (From the Heart of a Worshiper) requires circumcision; a cutting away.

WORSHIP is GOD-CENTERED. There can be no restraint or resistance if you are going to give God ALL that you have in order for him to respond to your gift of WORSHIP. Psalms 16:119 (KJV) tells us, "In HIS presence is fullness of joy and at his right hand are pleasure forever more." When one is in the presence of God there is completeness; there is no room for more; there is balance in every area needed. In HIS presence, you become full to overflowing; Worship, in its truest form, is NOT Burger King where you can "have it your way." WORSHIP requires complete concentration. WORSHIP (in its bona fide and unquestionable form) requires one to put forth effort because the common goal is to touch God!

WORSHIP requires dedication. It has to be based on commitment regardless of what has gone on, is going on, or will happen in a person's life. God still deserves to be WORSHIPPED! In the natural, you would not give a worn or used-up gift to the President, so why do you have the "that-a-do" attitude in presenting your gift of WORSHIP to the one True King of Kings, and Lord of Lords? There are a lot of replicas of Worshipping God, but the truth is, the heart is FAR from what is being said with the mouth.

If anyone is going through the motions of Worship in an effort to appear Holy and being a Worshiper before man, then that person is in grave danger of being reprimanded severely. God has no respecter of persons; as he dealt harshly with the Pharisees for their hypocrisy (as they went through the motions of following the law of God), he would be unfair if he accepted just anything from you. It must be real! References: Matthew 15:7-9; Mark 7:5-7 (KJV).

God is not accepting just anything merely because the word, "WORSHIP" is attached to it. God gave us all HIS best (in the person of his only begotten son, Jesus, the Christ; the anointed one), and he wants, deserves, and is settling for

NOTHING less than sincere, unfeigned WORSHIP!

God does not need your Worship to complete him; he is already complete, but he wants True Worshipers (which leads me to think there are those who contrive and present false and insincere Worship under the disguise of it being genuine). There are many who perform as if presenting God with his or her best gift when, often, the real underlying motive is simply to pull on God because he is capable of meeting needs and able to answer prayers. God must be WORSHIPPED because (to name a few reasons), he is Sovereign, Omnipresent, Omnipotent, Omniscient, and Transcendent.

The Full Life Study Bible, King James Version, Copyright 1992, under the study Worship (pg. 730) states: "The English word "worship" is derived from an Old English word, "worthship." This means God is WORTHY of our "ACTS" of WORSHIP that points or directs us to how great he is both in heaven and on the earth. It is important to really grasp this statement regarding worship and then go forward Worshipping God to the absolute fullest and not as something routinely done. We are to consider it as a privilege and an honor to WORSHIP such a God; not by force, indirection, promised positions, or what God can do for you (wrong motives). WORSHIP should be done because of an unwavering love for, and to HIM, both in-house and other ways mentioned, expressing PURE WORSHIP! Selah.

CHAPTER 9 – HUNGER AND THIRST FOR WORSHIP

If you are to be the Worshipers whom God is seeking, your quest must be insatiable. There must be an on-going fervor, a passion for CHRIST to saturate the heart, mind, soul, and spirit as you, the believer, allow the sweet fragrance of WORSHIP to fill your nostrils with God's incomparable aroma; until you WORSHIP with an EXTENDED, broader perspective, you will continue being limited in your experience and will also continue to be timid when Worshipping. To go to that place of Extended Worship (From the Heart of a Worshiper), it is necessary to redefine your past perceptions of what WORSHIP really is, and then be willing to delve deeper into the roots of it as defined and outlined in the Holy Scriptures.

When mentioning WORSHIP, and in an attempt to get others to WORSHIP, John 4:24 (KJV), is often quoted: "They that worship him must worship him in spirit and in truth." I believe this to be true, in its context, but do you believe it is speaking of the human spirit? Many theologians interpret this to mean that to WORSHIP in spirit and truth means to have a certain type of attitude that is right before God. What is your take on it? I choose the latter.

In researching, studying, praying, and meditating on WORSHIP, I see "Worshipping in truth" as both a doctrinal truth, based on principles taught then acted upon by one's belief, and also as being based on sincerity and genuineness of heart. Many times Worship is attempted to be forced when, in essence, all that needs to be done is to allow it to flow in the fullest interpretation of what is on the "inside" of the person.

When you consider hunger, you think of a desire to partake or something that you may crave. To thirst is to be deprived of the liquids the body needs to refrain from dehydration. To stay hydrated, one must supply the body with a sufficient amount of liquids, preferably water. On the Spiritual side, the same principle can be applied. If you are to go to the highest dimension of Extended Worship (From the Heart of a Worshiper), your push must be to learn, then put into practice, the "overall" constituents of Worship; not to isolate, diminish, nor lump it in the norm as being, "just a slow song" (as I keep reiterating).

You have got to hunger and thirst to KNOW God in all areas; ask him to, "Fill My Cup, Lord." This is beautifully demonstrated in the song pinned by Richard Blanchard with that title. These are the words:

Like the woman at the well I was seeking For things that could not satisfy;

And then I heard my Savior speaking:

"Draw from my well that never shall run dry."

Fill my cup Lord; I lift it up, Lord!

Come and quench this thirsting of my soul; Bread of heaven, Feed me til I want no more Fill my cup, fill it up and make me whole!

There are millions in this world who are craving The pleasures earthly things afford;

But none can match the wondrous treasure That I find in Jesus Christ my Lord.

So, my neighbor, if the things this world gave you Leaves hungers that won't pass away,

*My blessed Lord will come and save you If you kneel to
Him and humbly pray:*

Fill my cup Lord; I lift it up, Lord!

*Come and quench this thirsting of my soul; Bread of
heaven, Feed me til I want no more Fill my cup, fill it up
and make me whole!*

This song epitomizes a hungry and thirsty
soul going hard after God. To go to Extended
Worship (From the Heart of a Worshiper), you
can no longer be satisfied with being lukewarm. I
am eternally grateful for those who are not just
standing in one place but are hungering and
thirsting for the ultimate, greatest, most perfect
(mature), supreme, and absolute position that is
attainable in WORSHIP in every Biblical way.

The cry from those hungry and thirsty for
Extended Worship must be: "O Lord, show me
thy glory." The yearning of the soul must be to
taste; to go beyond "feelings" of the physical
"ACTS" of Worship and touch with the heart; to
see, with the inner "Spiritual eyes" the admiration
and wonderment of a well-deserved God as your
concept and application of Worship increases.

My desire is for all to go after this extended

place in Worship. Because many have not sought after the "whole" package of Worship, the standard has been that of a lackadaisical state both in the "ACT" of Worship and sadly, often, in LIFESTYLE because the latter was not traditionally considered to be Worship. There needs to be; must be, a sincere and intense desire to grow so that the manifestation of God Himself will be evident to His people in every form. My desire is for all to go after this extended place in Worship. Because many have not sought after the "whole" package of Worship, the standard has been that of a lackadaisical state.

God wants his people to Worship him, but he wants it to be performed with all your being so that there is nothing lacking, broken, nor omitted. He wants it complete as you experience, through your way of both "LIVING AND "ACTS" of Worship, what Extended Worship (From the Heart of a Worshiper) entails, and because he DESERVES IT!

CHAPTER 10 - NEWS THAT YOU CAN USE

If you are to grasp and hold on to the fact that there IS a significant difference between PRAISE AND WORSHIP, then your thought patterns must change as concentration is directed towards keeping the two in their proper and respective places. In ALL cases, ORDER is the mainstay of the day, and the Holy Spirit is the orchestrator of ANY service. When in Praise and Worship services, unless HE decides to move straight into WORSHIP, Praise should be continued until all of "self" is totally exhausted.

I say, "self," because even though it is in the word that "God inhabits the Praises of His people," Praise is still a SELF-CENTERED action whereby anyone, and even inanimate things, are commanded to give praises to Him. Because it is, if you will, "SELF-GRATIFYING," all of wanting to give thanks to God should be expressed; the congregation should have the chance during this specific timeframe to do so and to do it in an orderly sequence as scripture mandates.

As Praise and Worship leaders, and those in

charge of that particular slot in the service, ample time needs to be allowed for Praise alone. No one should attempt to rush directly into WORSHIP in an attempt to "speed up the service" before having given the congregation adequate time to thank God for the things, acts, and kindnesses he has shown.

I believe that PRAISE prepares the people to go farther into the unveiling of God's glory. I caution you here, however, and remind you that it is through WORSHIP that the Spirit answers the love that is exhibited first by your lifestyle, then by openly loving on a "one-of-a-kind God." You enter into "sweet" communion through the "ACT" of WORSHIP with God as you drink in all of his righteousness. Worship transcends time, space, problems, self, and gives you a brief glimpse of eternity present and future! PRAISE, on the other hand, allows EVERYONE breathing to be a participant; it does not require a relationship or actually "knowing" God.

Because the ultimate intent is to go to the Throne Room, you must NOT stop a service with just Praise unless, without a doubt, the Holy Spirit changed the direction. Why should PRAISE precede WORSHIP? Praise, according to "Ethel 101," is as John the Baptist was before the coming of Jesus, an "antecedent, or forerunner;" and, thus, it should be exhausted before moving on to the HIGHEST form of PRAISE, which is WORSHIP.

You Praise in order to get HIS attention since he "inhabits your praises, but the main goal, the final destination is to WORSHIP HIM; not just patty-caking, getting your shout on, but deep, penetrating WORSHIP that is done so sincerely that God will respond to the love bestowed upon him just for WHO he is and not for WHAT he has done. He wants to become your "exclusive" lover and will NOT share his place with anyone; as stated before, God does NOT need our WORSHIP to complete him, but he DOES want it, and he wants NOTHING less than AUTHENTIC WORSHIP!

"News That You Can Use!" This saying was borrowed from our own Bishop Jimmie C. Clark, Jr., Wings of Deliverance Tabernacle Holiness Church, Ft Wayne, IN.

CHAPTER 11 – WORSHIP IS NOT GENDER ORIENTED

There is nothing more beautiful than to be in a setting whereby the men of God are Worshipping God and actually taking the lead. This section is being written to remind them that WORSHIP is NOT gender-oriented.

I allude to this because I have noticed that when it comes to the arena of WORSHIP, (and I am referring now to touching God through a person's intimacy with him, and not referencing lifestyle, love of others, etc., but the "ACT" of WORSHIP). It is painfully apparent that, at times, some men will sit idly by being bystanders while 90% of the women in the sanctuary are approaching God through their WORSHIP; this is because, for whatever reason, the men seem to be unable to engage in it openly and freely.

Many sit and gaze in utter amazement as if to say, "What in the world are they doing?" Please, please, know that God EXPECTS, and WANTS so badly for you, the men, to WORSHIP him with the same vigor, reverence, love, and honor that those of the opposite sex are doing. He wants the men to forget how you might appear if on your faces before him; forget about WHO might be sitting next to you; forget that the suit being worn might be a Michael Kors, Gianni Versace, or a Giorgio Armani. God is seeking WORSHIPPERS!

In earlier years, I, along with other believers, would go to Joe Louis Arena, Detroit, MI, to conferences held by Apostle Fredrick K. Price, Kenneth Copeland, Jerry Sevelle, and their wives. Before each session, there would be such dynamic PRAISE, followed by Heavenly WORSHIP where, judging from the outward participation, it appeared that the men thought nothing about weeping before the Lord in sheer delight, and did it openly as they went from jubilant Praise to "touch-the-throne" Worship!

I was blessed to see those men of God of every race, color, and creed going forth and not being concerned about their persona, or what anyone might be thinking about their actions. All I could think was, "This is what God is seeking from his MEN!" I am directing this question specifically to the men reading this book: "Have you short-changed God in your WORSHIP?" If so, when, and for what reason?

God is waiting for the MEN of God, those who have that personal relationship with him, to take their rightful places as the "pacesetters" in Worship and not waiting to follow. He wants men to come out of their comfort zone, embarrassed state, or just plain not interested state and allow him to rejuvenate each of you in Praise (but especially in Worship) since this is the section about which I am writing.

God wants complete and total surrender as each of you Godly men move outside of yourselves and into the presence of God to experience a meaningful, and lasting experience in this Extended Worship. God does not want just the physical side of it, but the most impactful part, and that is the place that when you spend time in his presence, your entire life is altered; never to be the same again.

Will you allow him to do this in you? Will you do as one of our Elders always say (Elder Darrell Caldwell), "Come out with your hands up" in total surrender; telling God to have HIS way as to how he wants to use you in this area? He is available, are you? You can touch him, will you? Extended Worship is NOT gender-oriented; it is available, but is not automatic; you have to want it. Do you?

CHAPTER 12 – WORSHIP IS NOT A FEELING OR ENTERTAINMENT

What exactly is your reason for WORSHIPPING? I wish I had a dollar for the times I have overheard statements like, "I am so glad I made it here today so that I can get something from God," when in actuality and truth, the statement should be, "Thank-you God, for allowing me to get here. I am so excited that today I will be able to GIVE to you through my WORSHIP." I say this with full assurance that, no one will EVER out-give God at any time and in any way.

It moves me to tears when I think of how selfish some are, declaring their never-failing, never-ending love for God, but when they come to the house, the first and primary thing on their minds seem to be, "What can you do for me today?" When you come with such an approach and attitude toward WORSHIP, know that you will leave feeling as empty as when you came because none of what "God" says about how HE should be Worshipped was your primary reason for being there, nor displayed.

The inner man groans in agony to see how much is being missed by not knowing what God expects in WORSHIP in a lot of areas, but specifically, on not knowing our part in all facets of it. WORSHIP is NOT, as later discussed, to make anyone FEEL good, (even though they WILL once that place has been reached), and is most definitely not for entertainment

When it comes to WORSHIP, so many find themselves wanting what they want, and doing whatever makes them happy, or feels good; sad to say, this has spilled over into the time that is allotted for God in the form of WORSHIP. If it doesn't "feel" good, or if you don't "feel" it, then you will not go after, and capture that place of oneness with God through participation.

WORSHIP is NOT intended to make anyone "feel" good as stated before, nor to be entertained, nor be led into a stupor of "emotion of the moment," and once service is over, the discussion becomes; "I sure did feel good!" In all my reading prior to, and at the onset of getting material together for this book, I found NOTHING in scripture to substantiate the fact that we worship for a "feeling." We say, "I sure did feel God today." I pose this to you, to meditate on and even research for your personal knowledge; can one actually "feel" GOD's presence, or, is it that what is taking place is your RESPONSE, by way of your feelings, to a heightened consciousness that God has shown up, and his powerfulness has set up residency in the atmosphere?

Ethel, 101: I contend that the RESIDUE is from his presence or, is what you "feel" taking place is your RESPONSE, by way of those feelings, a heightened consciousness that God has shown up, and his powerful presence has set up residency in the atmosphere? I stand on this statement because I dare to believe if one ever actually "felt" HIM, the impact would be too much for anyone to handle and live to talk about it; similar to when Moses, in Exodus 33:18-23 (NIV), asked God to show him his glory. Scripture lets us know that the Lord did allow his goodness to show up in front of Moses, and he did declare his name as Lord. He went on to tell Moses that because of WHO he was, he could have mercy on whom he willed, and compassion on whom he decided, but he would NOT allow him to see his face because no one could see it and live.

Verses 21-23 of the same text states; "There is a place near me where you may stand on a rock, and when my glory passes by, I will put you in a cleft in the rock and cover you with my hand until I have passed by, then I will remove my hand, and you will see my back, but my face must not be seen." I maintain that God is too powerful for the natural eye, and your bodies too fragile to receive the FULL impact of his visitation. My consensus is that the "after effect" of his presence is what causes you to "feel" him as is often said.

When it comes to WORSHIP, being an onlooker seems to be more comfortable for some, and thus, it is treated as a spectator sport, but in truth, it is GOD who is the spectator as he sits waiting, often, in utter frustration, for TRUE WORSHIP to manifest itself. Because God is waiting, you should never resort to being an observer in WORSHIP; you need to make a concerted effort always to be an ACTIVE participant.

Many people, for lack of knowing differently, come to church for the "emotional" high that tradition has associated with WORSHIP. The actions are similar (as I have been told), to what a person is seeking who uses drugs and keeps using them until they are addicted in an attempt to reach that place of the initial high.

Try as they might, however, it is not achieved and, when it does not happen, (because they are never able to reach that original 100% high), they become addicted. Likewise, when the "emotional high" he or she is seeking does not happen in the service, this is when the blame- game begins, and statements are made like; "The Praise and Worship team sure was off today; the preacher sure didn't have a good word for us;" never once turning the spotlight inward to SELF to take inventory of why nothing was right in the assessment of the service.

Scripture does not state that WORSHIP is structured around the desires of "any" person. It has to be, at ALL times, God-centered, and God-ordained! TRUE WORSHIP is about pleasing God. Paul wrote in: Galatians 1:10 (KJV): "Do I seek to please men? For if I still pleased men, I would not be a servant of Christ." Here Paul is expounding on the fact that your pursuit in WORSHIP should NOT be about man, but toward God and ALL our energy should be toward that end and NOT about any other, not even self.

If you are to attain EXTENDED WORSHIP (From the Heart of a Worshiper), this attitude has to change. If it remains the same, then your WORSHIP will have no real meaning, no spiritual impact, and without a shadow of a doubt, will not be sufficient, nor admissible to HIM. I can hear God screaming in my spirit: "Take me OUT of the manger as a baby. See me in my FULLNESS, see me as the crucified, then RISEN SAVIOR. I require total commitment; I require a daily walk in Holiness; I desire to see an EFFECTUAL change in the lives of my people as they move to the dimension I have set for them in WORSHIP."

Much has been said thus far in this book, but please take to heart the following statement and accept it for ALL that it is worth: "To attempt to WORSHIP God the way you want is the highest form of disrespect for WHO he truly is. He is NOT going to continue to allow the people who claim to know and love him operate in this manner."

It is time to want more; NOT of God, because when you received Jesus, you received HIS fullness; but you CAN be ever-progressing, ever-seeking to perfect, to become more mature in the things of God, particularly in WORSHIP. It is time, right now, to ask God to reveal to you what the elements of True, Authentic, Pure, God-centered Christian WORSHIP is, as it relates to YOU individually. I asked, and he gave me the revelation that WORSHIP is forever; it is in EVERYTHING that a TRUE BELIEVER says and does. It is the fundamental character of the Christian's life. It is the prevailing theme of God's word.

It is a verb; it DEMANDS action on your part. When your WORSHIP is real, you are telling God that your very life is HIS in every area; not one thing is kept or hidden from him. WORSHIP tells God that you give him honor in ALL that you do.

Worship tells God that you give him honor in ALL that you do. You must: "choose" to WORSHIP with all that lies within because it is dear to your heart in lifestyle, acts of presentation, constant consecration, and reverence, as all is bestowed upon God freely. It is the "TOTALITY of your being." The time is now to WORSHIP and openly present the BEST you have, not for ulterior reasons, but to be given exclusively, for ONE single purpose, and that is to TOUCH God in the Throne room.

As more revelation and understanding is imparted regarding WORSHIP, you will come to realize that it is God's revelation TO you which, in turn, demands a response FROM you. In this place of WORSHIP, you will totally abandon your will and engage yourself in his will.

There is NO compromising in PURE WORSHIP. It is ALL on God's terms!

You have a God who waits for your WORSHIP and, oh, what a loss it would be when, because man was more important than he, God would suddenly and without warning, decide to shut up HIS bowels of compassion because of a lackadaisical attitude towards WORSHIP. As Worshipers, it is of the utmost importance to study the scriptures to know, without a doubt, how God wants and expects WORSHIP to be presented to him along with listening to, and then following, the Holy Spirit's direction.

Instead of operating in the often mundane tradition of man-made rules from whatever the source, you should do it in agreement with God's will. It is time to refrain from following the commands of men. Mark 7:7 (KJV), states:

"Howbeit in vain do they worship me, teaching for doctrines the commandments of men." When WORSHIP is not given God's way it is in vain; just a performance for man and what a sad, sad, position to find oneself.

Author's disclaimer: I am by no stretch of the imagination stating that everyone has to WORSHIP identically; to answer some questions that might be in the minds of many relating to "HOW to WORSHIP," I have compiled a short list to show a variety of ways it is done. Remember, it is PERSONAL, but always in order!

In Worship, some will:

Lift hands as they bless the Lord;

Stand in complete astonishment as God transmits love upon his people;

Stand or sit completely still and quiet; lips moving, but no audible sounds being heard. The Worshiper is letting go and letting God; being relaxed and comfortable in his presence;

Bowing or kneeling before him. This is in order; don't be afraid nor ashamed to lay prostrate before him.

Caution to all Worshipers: There will be times when people, even those closest to you, might not understand your WORSHIP, but as long as you KNOW God does, continue to do it decently and in order. God is NOT in a box! He loves a mix! He loves variety!

Since the "ACT" of Worship can be expressed in different ways, those in charge of a service, (not talking about your private Worship here), should never try to pre-guess the way the Spirit will move just because He moved a certain way at another time. We are not to assume someone is not in Authentic Worship; just be OPEN to His move. You are not to ever allow WORSHIP to become "traditional." It is time to rid yourselves of the mindset that "it must be your way or the highway" attitude. It is NOT your WORSHIP; it is God's, and this way of thinking has no place in ANY WORSHIP service!

Whether WORSHIP is in the home, or in the sanctuary, it should ALWAYS be done with respect and reverence for God. Isaiah 6:1-3 (KJV). Many try to bypass this, but WORSHIP is in vain when you know you have committed deliberate and willful sin and fail to repent; TRUE repentance precedes WORSHIP; Isaiah 64:6

(KJV): "Our righteousness are as filthy rags." When our WORSHIP is devoid of any hypocrisy or phoniness, it will cause you to have a sense of responsibility toward God; Isaiah 6:5-13 (KJV). When WORSHIP is EXTENDED and comes from the heart of a Worshiper, there is no desire or need for pats on the back for living a life of Holiness and responsibility. Romans 12:1-3 (KJV), lets us know that "It is just our REASONABLE service."

If God is going to be pleased with your gifts of WORSHIP, then you must migrate from "emotion of the moment" to flowing in God's will. You must move from how intellectual you are, how many gifts and talents you possess, from being a sideliner watching, to being a functioning participant; one who is so grateful just to be allowed to WORSHIP such a deserving God who is the ONLY one who holds this position of esteem. You should consider it an honor and a privilege to WORSHIP him!

In researching material for this book, I ran across some profound information shared with me on the topic with my long-time friend and spiritual sister, Reverend Bernice Jones; (some of the original wording has been paraphrased) from her paper on Worship Elements, which is included and discussed in the next chapter.

CHAPTER 13 – WORSHIP ELEMENTS

AGAPE:

Unconditional love - People who operate in the element of unconditional love don't get to pick and choose "if" they are going to love; it is a command from God, a must. This type of love is a prerequisite to all that is available. It is the very core, the foundation upon which WORSHIP is established.

Worship is a choice, but love must not be just a word; it must be action. It is a "God principle." You are to love both God AND people with everything within you. You are to love Him more than the very air that you breathe. You are to love Him more than your "necessary food!"

AMAZEMENT:

You are to always be in amazement at the wonders of God. When in the presence of God, never take him for granted. God is to be adored reverently. Psalms 33:6 (NIV): "By the word of the Lord the heavens were made, their starry host by the breath of his mouth."

Yes, be amazed, but get him out of the confines of your "finite" minds. He is way too stupendous to be limited, so allow HIS Worship to be Expanded (From the Heart of a Worshiper); you!

SEE BEYOND WHAT YOU SEE:

Worship is to see beyond what you "see." You should desire to go to the fullest place when Worshipping. Job: 37:33 (NIV): "The Almighty is beyond our reach and exalted in power; in his justice and great righteousness, he does not oppress. Worship is the "entire package."

ADORE REVERENTLY:

To show reverence is to be done with everything within you and at all times; it is not optional. While bowing, singing, lifting of the hands are forms of the "ACTS" of Worship, adoring reverently far exceeds any of these actions.

Adoring reverently taps loudly at the very center of the heart and its position. It causes one to examine "what" or "who" you have been Worshipping all your lives, knowingly or unknowingly, because everyone Worships something or someone.

Don't be afraid to love on God; to audibly say how much you love him, to reverence him, to adore him. He can handle the millions who Worship him. Psalms 29:2 (NN): "Ascribe to the Lord the glory due his name; worship the LORD in the splendor of his holiness."

CHAPTER 14 – WORSHIP IS KNOWING GOD

If you are ever to reach the pinnacle of WORSHIP which God desires for each of you as believers, you will need to build that personal, intimate, relationship with Him. How can one effectively WORSHIP a God who is unfamiliar; one whom you know nothing about outside of what you have heard said by your momma or daddy, your Pastor, or a family member or friend? It is good to hear the expressions of others as to what he means to them, but you need to know what he means to you! You need to spend time alone with HIM, not asking for anything, just listening and learning to hear HIS voice.

When you really get to know God for yourself, WORSHIP will touch the inner part of your being. It will free you from anything, anyone objectionable, undesirable, or who might be a form of distraction that hinders you from surrendering to the perfect will of God.

I have had the sad experience of thinking more highly of myself than I ought. I know none of you readers have ever been there, but I promised to be totally honest in this writing. When I realized that God hated this in me, especially being a WORSHIPER, this made it painfully clear that none of my WORSHIP should, nor ever would be about me. This realization revolutionized my entire outlook on the subject. If you will just be honest and then get serious with God, you will see him change you into a PURE Worshiper also.

He knows what he wants from each of you, and you know something; he is going to get it! He, through his Spirit, let me know that he had always wanted my deepest WORSHIP, even before I was formed in my mother's womb. It was confirmed in prophecy to me by Elder DeLoach who had come to my home church, Wings of Deliverance, to run a revival.

God had revealed to him how to go to the depths of WORSHIP. One night after a service so powerful in Worship that everyone just lingered, sobbing before God, he said, "God told me to tell you that you were chosen for such a time as this. That he wanted you to stop being afraid to go where he wants to take you in WORSHIP and, if you will be obedient, he will cause the demons themselves to have to leave the sanctuary because of GOD'S powerful presence through my WORSHIP."

I listened as he kept speaking and told me that I would have to be willing to be ridiculed, talked about, ignored, and all that goes along with naysayers who do not understand what God was going to do in and through me in my "WORSHIP." I did not get his entire prophetic message until one of my Spiritual sons, Shawn Davis, came to me and said, "Mom, did you get all that he said?" He then gave me the paper where he had written it all down; that was another defining moment and the beginning of an awesome walk in TRUE WORSHIP for me!

I took a personal inventory of Ethel; (no one else), and seeing areas which I did not like, repented and gave it ALL to God. I began to eat the word; fast, pray, and honestly let God know that I was now "completely" available for him to use me (without fear of reprisal and reactions from anyone, or lack thereof), to WORSHIP MY GOD!

In dreams, visions, and prophecies, God let me know that he despised WORSHIP that was self-centered; if it was going to be pleasing to HIM, and not MAN, it had to be God-centered (cannot stress this enough); whatever I did for him I was to have NO hidden motives; the thoughts and intents had to be undiluted, unmixed, free from foreign elements of pride, not doing it for man's approval and "atta-boys." He wanted it all for himself. He wanted what was hidden on the inside. He wanted the internal so it would spill over to the external. He was DEMANDING my PURE HEART! Bless God!

An important message to note as you continue reading: "God is weary and completely fed up with man's form of WORSHIP where the concern is so centered around fashion, talent, gifts, and style; yes, these are essential in the proper setting, but Extended Worship (From the Heart of a Worshiper) has to exceed any of these because God is concerned with the EPITOME of WORSHIP which comes directly from the heart.

Enough "flesh" has been on parade. It is time out for "show-and-tell" in WORSHIP. God has to be the PRIMARY focal point and is settling for nothing less. Because of many variables, many have settled because they did not want to lose their best singers, musicians, long-standing members, but today, right now, God is saying: "ENOUGH!" He WILL NOT be found accepting tainted WORSHIP dressed up in learned habits and traditions, then presenting it to him. NO MORE! Selah.

CHAPTER 15 – THE SUSTAINING FORCE OF WORSHIP

The inclusion of this section in the book may be questionable to many, but as the Spirit of God began to reveal the depth of EXTENDED WORSHIP (From the Heart of a Worshiper) to me, little did I know that I would later face the greatest challenge of my life and that it would be WORSHIP that would be one of the key elements that would be a lifesaver for me.

The bodily attack started with me becoming, seemingly out of nowhere, so fatigued that it was next to impossible to·do normal walking, and especially going up and down steps, performing everyday duties (which included personal hygiene). It hurt even to have clothes touch my body. The only time I was able to tolerate the excruciating pain, was when I WAS IN PRAISE, but most definitely in the 'ACT" of WORSHIP, whether at home or in the sanctuary.

I was unable to even dress myself, but thank God for a husband who was not only there, but was willing to do whatever was necessary to get me through this ordeal. WORSHIP, for sure, would prove to be that formidable force that would keep me from yielding and giving up during this problematic, intense, and stressful period.

A long, tedious regiment of tests were ordered to medically find out why I was tired to the degree of being almost bedridden. They began with taking blood samples to determine if the cause was due to anemia. Anemia was ruled out, but there was still no apparent reason for the tiredness and pain. With no progress being made as to what was happening in my body, my PCP, Primary Care Physician, said I was in "dire" need of more extensive tests than merely drawing vials of blood, and I was then referred to a Hematologist.

After more tests, the specialist found my blood level was dangerously low; instead of the normal pints for a woman which is 9-10, I barely had three (3); something was using up my blood supply, but so far, there was no knowledge of the source. My blood type was verified and then I was asked if I would submit to what they called, a "blood infusion" (I don't know the difference from a transfusion except this one was more costly.) I agreed to get it and weeks later, another checkup was given and my blood level was NOT rising; something was still causing me to lose blood, but nothing definitive had been established as its source. The Hematologist concluded that something internal had to be absorbing the blood and then ordered a colonoscopy.

Author's sidebar: "To anyone who might be struggling with going to natural doctors, please accept this advice, if you have a prolonged condition which has attached itself to your body and, after FIRST believing God to manifest his healing in you and it does NOT happen (in the natural), take the next step of Faith and go to a physician." God gets no glory in believers dying because they are not willing to see a doctor. Jesus was the healer, but Luke, who was called the "beloved physician' walked with Jesus as one of his disciples. As you go through adversity, especially healing, you must never forget that it is JESUS, the CHRIST, who manifests healing and causes wholeness to take place.

The colonoscopy was administered and anyone who has ever taken one knows that normally a person comes from under the procedure with little or no knowledge of what has transpired; however, such was not the case with me. I went in WORSHIPPING, and when I came from under the anesthesia, I heard the words: "Cecal Mass." I saw my friend, Evangelist Eunice Taylor, who had gone with me, my husband, Terry, and one of our sons, Ron, talking in the hallway in 'hushed" tones and my son was crying as she consoled him. I called out to them and asked, "Where is the mass?"

At first, they pretended not to hear me, but I kept saying the same tiring and finally I was told that they had found a mass (cancer) in my colon. No, I did not jump up and down with the diagnosis and began quoting healing scriptures, but I did know that this was a fight, and I intended to WIN.

I started doing replays as to why in the months prior to the diagnosis my WORSHIP had become so intense and then I recalled Prophetic words spoken to me by my late Pastor, Jimmie C. Clark, Sr., Mother Marilyn Clark, and my friend, the late Evangelist Bobbie Hudson. At different times they all would say, "it is well," or "this is not unto death, but to bring glory and honor to God." They were saying all of this even though NOT ONE person who encouraged me knew of the actual diagnosis given at the time they spoke life into me.

This was February, 2010. The attending Oncologist wanted to perform surgery immediately, but I told him I needed some time and would get back with him. I began to seek the Lord as to what to do; I told the surgeon if it was not gone the next time an ultrasound was performed I would set a date to have the surgery. I was given another ultrasound a month later, and it was still there. As I came to terms with what was ahead, I knew I had to be at a place in my inner being and remain there if I was going to be victorious in this battle.

The diagnosis pushed me to know WORSHIP in a greater, more in-depth way than I had ever known or experienced. Yes, I had been a Worshiper since my conversion, but I had only touched the surface in seeing it extended; the cancer took me to a point where I learned that EXTENDED WORSHIP was so much more encompassing than how it had been perceived; this venture proved to be a real learning experience as to the power of "real" Worship without limits!

I was opened up to WORSHIP with an

understanding that was rising from the most basic structure of me as an individual. I came to realize WORSHIP was an essential element to so many areas in my life, and walking me through this was one journey that would prove, for certain, that Worship is much bigger than just a "slow" song. WORSHIP was, and is, meant to touch EVERY part of your life, and should have both influence AND power.

When the Spirit instructed me to place this section in the book, I honestly asked: "Will anyone associate a diagnosis of cancer as a 'key' element involved in one's healing process and deeper relationship of Worship?"

In the weeks leading up to the actual surgery, more extensive tests were ordered to be sure the mass had not metastasized; thanks be to God it had not spread. The next step was to arrive at the best non-intrusive method of surgically removing it. While all of this was going on, I concentrated on what had gotten me through many adversities, and that was my intimate, one-on-one time of WORSHIP with my God. It was ingrained in my mind, body, soul, and spirit. I realized that to get through this, I not only had to think about it, but I also had to MAINTAIN it! I had to know that it was not a secondary substitute trying to emulate the original which God had laid out; it was more. It was powerful. It was NOT counterfeit, and even though many would try to duplicate it, it was empty of any FALSE virtue and not hypocritical in any shape, form, or fashion.

WORSHIP proved to be the true embodiment of what I needed in my fight with cancer and was powerful as I faced the uncertainty of not knowing the outcome, even with surgery. I can honestly say I was at TOTAL peace because WORSHIP had literally become my SUSTAINING force! When the pain was of such a magnitude that I would have to place my hand over my mouth to muffle the screams (to keep from disturbing my husband), I yet held onto that inner WORSHIP.

There were times when the tears would silently roll down my face, but I held close the words of the song "Great and Mighty is Our God," reassuring me of how loving and adorable this Great and Mighty God was and letting me know that no matter where I was at this time, I had to continue to trust and believe the word he had given; that RHEMA word came after an intense, personal Worship in my bed.

He protected my mind and from that point on, never let me lose hope. The scripture God placed in my spirit was, Isaiah 26:3 (KJV): "Thou wilt keep him in perfect peace, whose mind is stayed on thee: because he trusteth in thee."

Until I went through the cancer ordeal, or test, I did not know or fully comprehend how one has to PUSH to stay at a place God has placed them. The struggle to remain at a stationary place proved to be somewhat difficult at times (when I was listening in the natural), and as I heard people talking and listened as many, even biological family members and church members perceived me to be "over the top" or just plain "losing it." There were even some who went on to say: "I was seeing this through rose-colored glasses, not thinking rationally, and not accepting what was happening to me." I heard, but I REFUSED to retreat!

A week before the actual surgery, two sisters, the late Fannie Beasley, and my twin, Hester Brown, flew from Florida to be my "caregivers" and stayed for five weeks. As we talked, I saw Romans 8:28 (NIV) come alive: "And we know that in all things God works for the good of those who love Him, who have been called according to his purpose." I loved him and had been called for HIS purpose, so I kept my WORSHIP. It became as much needed as a lifeguard to a drowning person. The weeks my sisters spent were priceless ones that I shall never forget. We laughed, cried, prayed, and Worshipped together; little did any of us know that the older one would go home to be with the Lord three years later.

As is normal procedure, I was told of the impending danger of any surgery, but this one in particular because it was determined that I would need to lose 40% of my colon. They would not know until actually performing the surgery if a colostomy bag would be required, or if I would have to undergo chemotherapy and, or radiation.

I give God praise that NONE of these were needed. God IS a faithful God! He not only brought me through the surgery but in record time since it had been predicted it would be approximately five hours. I told them it would be three; one for the Father, Son, and Holy Spirit; it was three! They said the hospital stay would be at least a week; I was home in three days. How awesome is trusting God? Trusting God is another form of EXTENDED WORSHIP!

In all that I went through, I make my boast in the Lord. I was hooked up for the pain drip of morphine, but I had determined not to take any, so I kept praying and Worshipping. When I was in the hospital, I took no pain medication. While recuperating for the next eight weeks, I took only three Extra-Strength Tylenol for pain. There was something working in three's for me! Hallelujah!

WORSHIP got me through situations where nothing and no one else could touch. God has NO respecter of persons; if you need him in what appears to be an impossible situation, get into Extended Worship (From the Heart of a Worshiper). It has been many years now, and God has remained FAITHFUL. Worship WAS indeed, my SUSTAINER both THEN, and even more so now, as I continue seeking more and more of his revelations on the subject of, "Extended Worship (From the Heart of a Worshiper)."

CHAPTER 16 – WORSHIP IS MY CREATIVE ABILITY

WORSHIP became creative for me when I started recognizing that when I was in that deep place with the Father, I could hear words, melodies, and rhymes. I must admit that initially, I thought I was just imagining things, but when it kept happening, I mentioned it to my sisters, and they reminded me that we all liked to write so I should at least jot down what I was hearing and that is what I did. A song was produced during the time of the physical attack, and by the Holy Spirit, the tempo and lyrics were given as I wrote:

"Thank You, Lord:"

Thank you, Lord today For all that's come my way; It's working for my good,
In every way it should, I thank you, Lord today,
For every trial you allowed to come my way, Oh, thank you, Lord
I thank you I do; I really do, Thank you, Lord, I thank you, Lord
For all, you've done for me.
(Vamp)
When the trials come, Oh, I thank you, When the storms arise, Lord, I yet thank you,

I thank you, Lord today,
For every trial you allowed to come my way, Oh,
thank you, Lord,
I do, I really do Thank you, Lord,
Thank you, Thank you, Thank you, Lord
For all you've done for me

Ethel L. Comer Copyright©: June 2010

MY JOURNEY

Since my journey on the WORSHIP trail, I know more and more, that each and every encounter you have with God might not be for you to share, but many times it is to make YOU cognizant of something that the Spirit has opened up just for you; however, the contents of this book are to be shared by way of publication so that others may explore the vastness of WORSHIP.

You who are reading this book, if you have found it to be TOTALLY contrary to what you have been accustomed to, it is INTENDED to be. However, do not reject its contents because I had to be obedient in writing exactly what, and how, the Spirit dictated. From its inception, I knew it would NOT be the frequently-used format of other writers nor written in a conventional way concerning WORSHIP, but it is "GOD" mandated, and Holy Spirit inspired, so it had to be the way the Spirit has given it to me.

I pray that you had a good journey in the reading of this book and that you have gained useful knowledge from its contents; knowledge that will free you to engage in free PRAISE, and especially for you to get into WORSHIP and know the fullness of it, and that you will know whatever you face in life, WORSHIP will sustain you, even during those bleakest moments; those times when Satan is putting up his best fight against you. When you are totally and wrongfully misunderstood, keep Worshipping and keep being involved as you allow your total being to be engrossed in WORSHIP!

If you will commit to doing this, your eyes will be opened as you become a discerner of what GOD is doing through the vehicle of WORSHIP. We all not only CAN but MUST be an intrinsic part of the move of God. He wants so much to endow us to the point of overflowing so that we may see AND experience him in his fullness and in the fullness of a PURE and AUTHENTIC WORSHIP! Selah.

EPILOGUE

Writing this book has been an honor. It has enhanced my understanding of PRAISE, WORSHIP, AND EXTENDED WORSHIP (From the Heart of a Worshiper), with primary emphasis on the latter to elevate the thinking to a greater dimension, and to relate to the awesome power of WORSHIP.

As discussed in the body of the book, when music is used as a means of bringing listeners into PRAISE, the goal is to lead them to a HIGHER form, which is WORSHIP, and WORSHIP should then touch the very heartbeat of God because it is God centered and never self-desired. It should always be about HIM, and what HE deserves, not because of what he can DO for you, but simply because of WHO he is!

It is my prayer that the contents of this book get into your heart and spirit as you know that this is the place God wants you to be; in a ready state of WORSHIP. When you "live" there, in this place of WORSHIP, those who are weak find strength. The sad are made joyful. Those wanting to give up realize they can make it. The sick are made well (naturally and spiritually), and those who are struggling find means of working things out, and if the season is over, strength is received to move on. If unable to forgive, forgiveness comes (because one cannot WORSHIP without forgiveness). Bad habits are also destroyed. All of these are attained in HIS manifested presence. Psalms 16:11 (ISV) lets us know: "You cause me to know the path of life in your presence is joyful abundance, abundance at your right hand there are pleasures forever." Selah.

NOTES

_____

_____

_____

_____

_____

_____

_____

_____

_____

_____

_____

_____

_____

_____

_____

_____

_____

_____

_____

_____

_____

ABOUT THE AUTHOR

Ethel L. Comer is an Evangelist; active member of the Wings of Deliverance Tabernacle Holiness Church, Ft. Wayne, In.; she ministers at Conferences and Seminars throughout many states. She is a retired professional and married to William (Terry) Comer; through a blended family, she is the mother of nine children, 23 grandchildren, and 10 great-grandchildren. She has had, and continues to have, a blessed life as she enjoys Extended Worship (From the Heart of a Worshiper). God Bless!

www.ingramcontent.com/pod-product-compliance
Lightning Source LLC
Chambersburg PA
CBHW052125090426
42741CB00009B/1958